Animal Tracks and Traces

by Mary Holland

Have you ever seen a skunk? A raccoon? Or an opossum? Many people haven't because these animals are active at night (nocturnal) when we are sleeping. Then they are asleep during the day when we are awake.

Wherever nocturnal animals go, they leave all kinds of traces. It's fun to go outside during the day and look for their signs. The tracks and other traces of animals may tell you who has been there, where they went, and what they did during the night.

When an animal walks in dirt, sand, mud, or snow, they leave tracks (or imprints of their feet) where they have stepped. Notice where you find tracks. Do they go along a stone wall? Are they near a stream? Do they cross a field? If they go from tree to tree, a squirrel may have made them.

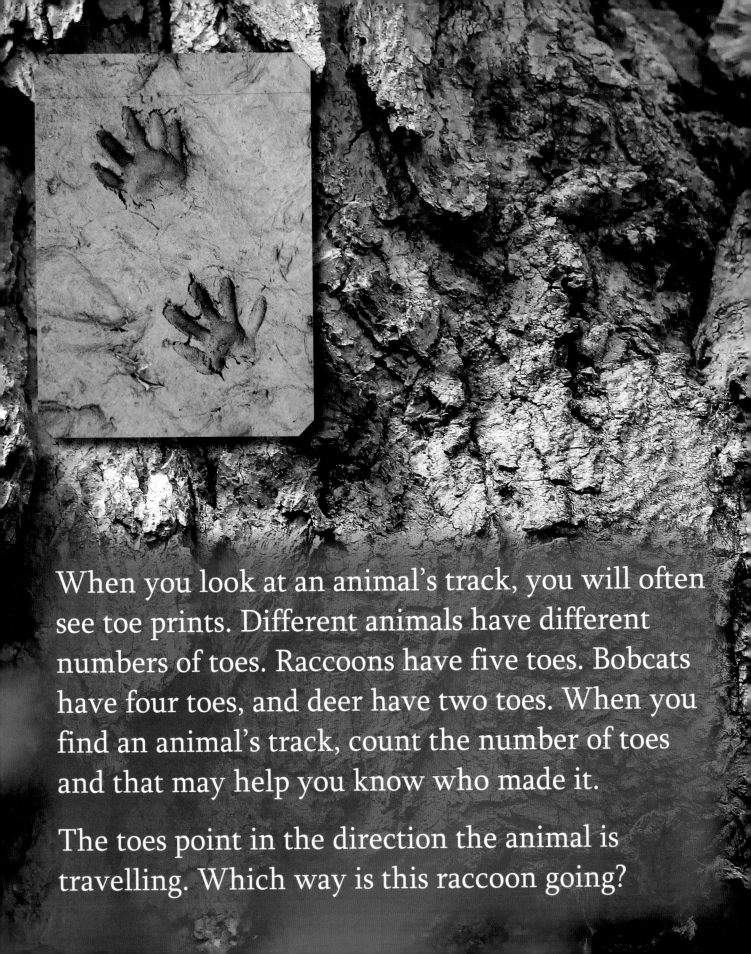

When you look at an animal's track, you will often see toe prints. Different animals have different numbers of toes. Raccoons have five toes. Bobcats have four toes, and deer have two toes. When you find an animal's track, count the number of toes and that may help you know who made it.

The toes point in the direction the animal is travelling. Which way is this raccoon going?

Most birds have four toes: three in front and one in the back. Many birds fly more than they walk, but wild turkeys walk more than they fly. Look for their tracks in the snow.

Do you like to go sledding? River otters do too! They lie down on their bellies, pick up their feet and slide down hills and across fields, leaving grooves in the snow. How many otters do you think sledded down this hill?

Tracks aren't the only signs that animals leave. Sometimes when an animal is eating something, it leaves marks where it has been eating. Moose eat tree bark. They scrape upwards on the trunk of a tree with their front, bottom teeth in order to remove the bark. The grooves a moose's teeth make are often very high on a tree, as moose are very tall!

Just like people, all animals have to pee and poop. Just like tracks, the poop (scat) of one kind of animal can look quite different from the scat of another animal. Weasel, fox and coyote scat is long and narrow, shaped like a finger. Deer, moose, mouse and rabbit scat is in the form of pellets. The bigger the animal, the bigger the pellets!

Many animals have their own area, or territory, where they find food to eat and where they raise a family. They often mark their territory by peeing and pooping on stumps and rocks. These are like signposts for other animals to smell and know who lives there.

Black bears mark their territory by scratching, rubbing, climbing on, and biting trees! They are leaving their scent on these trees for other bears to smell.

When an animal lies down to rest, it often mats down the grass or melts the snow it lies on. Can you find a coyote's bed in this picture?

Many animals build homes to raise their young. Some dig burrows into the ground, some live in hollow trees, and some build their home with sticks, stones, mud, or plants. Some homes, like beaver lodges, are very easy to find. Others, like fox dens, are often hidden and harder to see.

Most birds raising a family only use their nest one time. By the end of the summer, there are many empty nests. Mice sometimes use empty bird nests as winter homes. They collect milkweed down, cattail fluff, or other insulating materials and make a roof for the nest. All winter they will stay warm and dry inside.

You can find tracks, scat, markings, feeding signs, and animal homes anywhere you live. Become an animal track and trace detective! Even if you don't see the animal itself, the signs that it leaves can tell you who lives near you, where they go, what they eat, and much, much more. What animal signs have you found? What signs have you left?

For Creative Minds

Who Has Eaten Here?

Match each animal to its food sign.

A.   Beavers cut down trees with their teeth and eat the bark.

B.   Red squirrels eat seeds in cones and the uneaten scales drop to form a pile (midden).

C.   Striped skunks dig little round holes in the ground looking for insects.

Answers: A2, B3, C1

Whose Track is This?

Match each animal with its track.

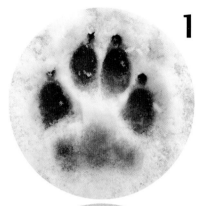

1

A white-tailed deer walks on two toenails.

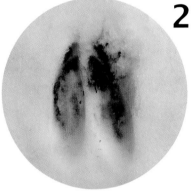

2

Dogs have four toes.

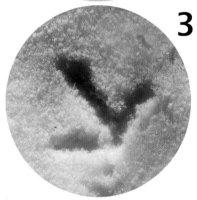

3

Fishers and other weasels have five toes.

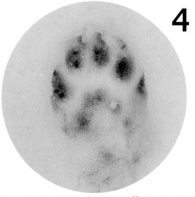

4

Birds have three toes in front and one in back.

Answers: Deer-2; Dog-1; Fisher-4; ruffed grouse-3

Animal Signs To Look For

Animals leave all kinds of signs that they have been there, not just tracks. Look for some of these other animal signs around you.

spider web

feather

cocoon

holes in leaves chewed by insects

bird-wing marks

bird nest

animal's home

skull

bald-faced hornet nest

frog eggs

owl pellet

scat

Other Animal Signs

Fly: Inside the round "ball" found on some goldenrod stems (gall) is a young fly waiting until spring to come out.

Beaver: Beavers mark their territory by building piles of mud and leaves (scent mounds). They leave their scent (castoreum) on the scent mound which tells other beavers to stay away.

Honey bee: Honey bees usually build their wax combs in tree cavities, but sometimes they build them out in the open.

Pileated woodpecker: Pileated woodpeckers drill big holes in trees looking for carpenter ants to eat.

To my favorite track detectives: Otis, Lily Piper and Leo—MH

Thanks to Hannah Gelroth, Director of School Programs and Teacher Professional Development at the Vermont Institute of Natural Science for verifying the accuracy of the information in this book.

Library of Congress Cataloging-in-Publication Data

Names: Holland, Mary, 1946- author.
Title: Animal tracks and traces / by Mary Holland.
Description: Mt. Pleasant, SC : Arbordale Publishing LLC, [2020] | Includes bibliographical references. | Audience: Ages 4-9 | Audience: Grades 2-3
Identifiers: LCCN 2019033032 (print) | LCCN 2019033033 (ebook) | ISBN 9781643517476 (hardcover) | ISBN 9781643517520 (trade paperback) | ISBN 9781643517827 (ebook other) | ISBN 9781643517728 (epub)
Subjects: LCSH: Animal tracks--Juvenile literature. | Animal behavior--Juvenile literature.
Classification: LCC QL768 .H65 2020 (print) | LCC QL768 (ebook) | DDC 591.47/9--dc23
LC record available at https://lccn.loc.gov/2019033032
LC ebook record available at https://lccn.loc.gov/2019033033

Lexile® Level: 610L
key phrases: animal behavior
Title in Spanish: *Las huellas y rastros de los animales*

Animals in this book include: female yellow-bellied sapsucker (title page), opossum, gray squirrel, raccoon, wild turkey, north American river otter, moose, white-tailed deer, red fox, black bear (on cover and inside text), coyote, beaver, white-footed mouse, and humans.

Bibliography:

Holland, Mary. *Naturally Curious: A Photographic Field Guide and Month-By-Month Journey Through the Fields, Woods, and Marshes of New England*. North Pomfret, VT: Trafalgar Square Books, 2010. Book.
Weber, Jen Funk. *Been There, Done That: Reading Animal Signs*. Mt. Pleasant, SC: Arbordale Publishing, 2016. Book.

Printed in China, November 2019
This product conforms to CPSIA 2008
First Printing

Arbordale Publishing
Mt. Pleasant, SC 29464
www.ArbordalePublishing.com